Body

A Quiz

Sarah Fleming

Contents

Body Beautiful

People have used human bodies as works of art for thousands of years. Sometimes people changed the way they looked to make them feel more beautiful. What made them feel more beautiful depended on where and when they lived. It still does.

The Chinese wrapped girls' feet up in bandages because small feet were fashionable.

This ancient Egyptian queen wore makeup that the ancient Egyptians found beautiful. It looks a lot like makeup people wear today.

When these women were between four and seven years old, their four small toes were folded under each foot, and then wrapped up. The wrappings were made tighter every day. Every few weeks they were given smaller shoes until their feet were no longer than four inches (10 cm).

AD 600–1900

Until the twentieth century, rich people from many **cultures** used to keep away from the sun. It was fashionable to have pale skin. Since the 1920s, having a suntan has become more fashionable.

In some cultures, people change the way they look so that others know more about them.

Definition
Culture: the customs and traditions of a people

Hindu women wear a red spot on their forehead to show that they are married.

War!

Not all body art is meant to be beautiful. Bodies can be decorated for other reasons:

- to please a person's gods
- to frighten away enemies
- for an event
- to frighten evil spirits

This man is painting his body. He has decorated it to tell a story from the past.

Body Painting

A

B

C

Match the photo to the reason for body painting.

1 for fun

2 to go to war

3 to be fashionable

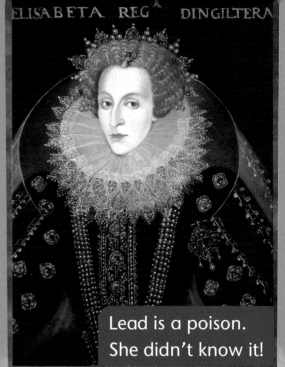

Lead is a poison. She didn't know it!

A–1 Some body painting is just for fun.

B–3 Queen Elizabeth I painted her face with white lead because it was fashionable to have pale skin.

C–2 Many different tribes paint themselves to go to war. These warriors are from Indonesia.

Makeup can be used to make you look and feel different.

Tattoos

Instead of just painting themselves, some people have their skin **tattooed**. Can you see:

- a tiger?
- 3 red flowers?
- a panda?
- 2 black panthers?

This man has had his whole body tattooed. He lives on a Scottish island in a hut and bathes in a river.

New Zealand Maori tattoos are called "moko."

Tattoos should be done by a professional to avoid infections and scarring. If a person changes his or her mind about a tattoo, removing it can scar his or her skin for life.

Tattoos have been found on ancient Egyptian mummies.

Body Shaping

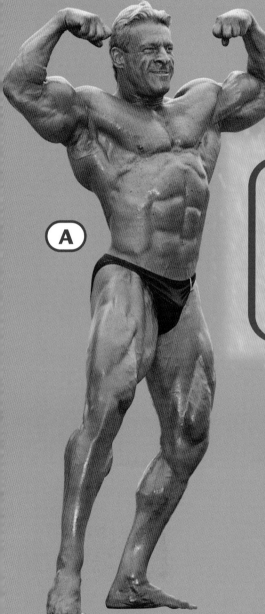

A

How do you think these people made their bodies look like this?

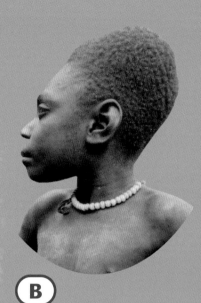

B

C

Answers

A Bodybuilders work out at the gym a lot. Some eat special diets. Some take pills that build up their muscles. If they take too many, the pills can make them very ill.

B Head Shaping

Babies in this tribe have their heads wrapped up tightly to make their skulls get longer as they grow up.

C Women add one ring at a time to slowly stretch their necks.

Necks get up to 15 inches (40 cm) long! However, the neck bones are no longer connected to each other. If the woman took the rings off, she would die.

Operations

A This woman has had operations on her face to look like an animal.

How do you think her face has been changed?

Which animal do you think she wants to look like?

B This woman has had operations on her face to make her look younger and prettier. How do you think her face has been changed?

Answers

A This woman has had her face changed to look like a leopard. She has had her eyes and cheeks reshaped. The color of her skin was changed, and her lips were made bigger.

B This woman has had many "face-lifts" to make her look younger.

She has also had eye lifts, a nose job, cheek implants, and had her lips made bigger. Her teeth have been made whiter and straighter. Her chin has been made smaller and her jaw reshaped.

Why do you think people want to look younger?

Scarring

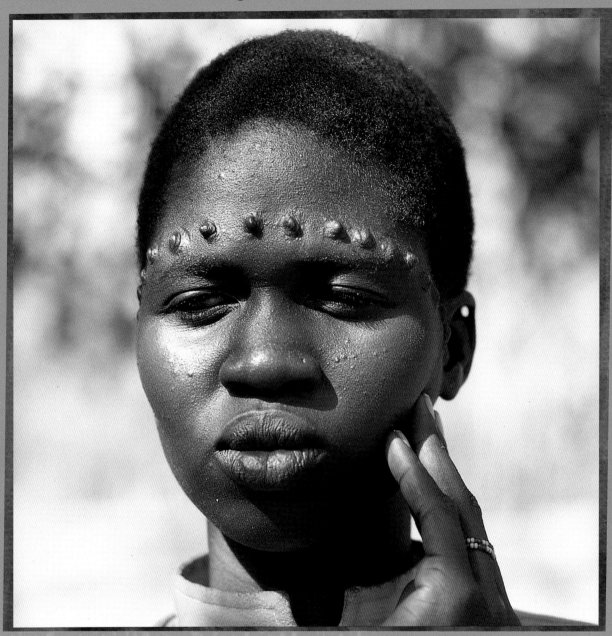

How do you think this woman made her skin look like this?

The bumps are made by cutting the skin. They can be made larger by rubbing the cuts with soil or grit as they heal.

Scarring is common in some cultures. Scars can be made for different reasons, such as to make a person look beautiful, to show how important a person is, or to give the person courage to go to war.

The scars in this body art have little stones in them to raise them higher.

Piercing

Making holes in a body is called piercing. The holes are used to wear jewelry.

Which part of the body do you think people have pierced most often?

Answer The ear

In some cultures, the bigger the holes in a person's ears, the more important the person is.

Ear-piercing has been popular all around the world for over five thousand years.

In ancient Rome, only rich people had their ears pierced.

Photo 1

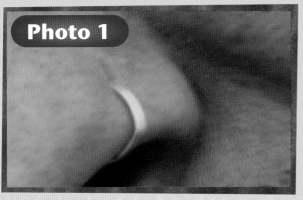

Photo 2

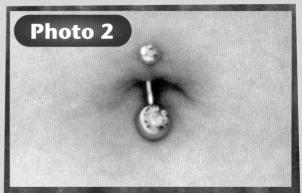

1 Where in the body is this piece of jewelry?

2 Which of the three pieces of jewelry, A, B, or C, is shown in photo 1?

4 Where in the body is this piece of jewelry?

5 Which of the three pieces of jewelry, D, E, or F, is shown in photo 2?

3 Which of the other pieces of jewelry could you use in the same part of the body?

6 Which of the other pieces of jewelry could you use in the same part of the body?

Photo 1 answers

1 The nostril.

2 A

3 You can wear A and B in the side of your nostril, but C, a bulli, is worn in the middle of the nose.

bulli

Photo 2 answers

4 The navel.

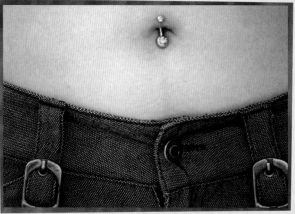

5 F

6 You can wear all of these in your navel.

When a navel hole is made, it can keep blood from getting to the skin around the navel. The skin dies and the jewelry falls out.

A navel piercing is long and deep. It takes five months for the hole to heal.

The Mouth

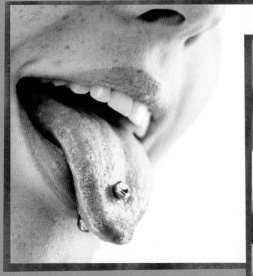

1 How long can it take for a tongue to stop bleeding after it has been pierced?

  A 1 week
  B 3 weeks
  C 6 weeks

2 Why did these 1930s movie stars have their back teeth taken out? Did they have to do it:

  A because they were rotten?
  B to make their cheeks look thinner?
  C to sell the teeth to their fans?

1—C It can take six weeks for your tongue to stop bleeding. During this time the wound can get infected.

2—B They had their teeth taken out to make their cheeks look thinner.

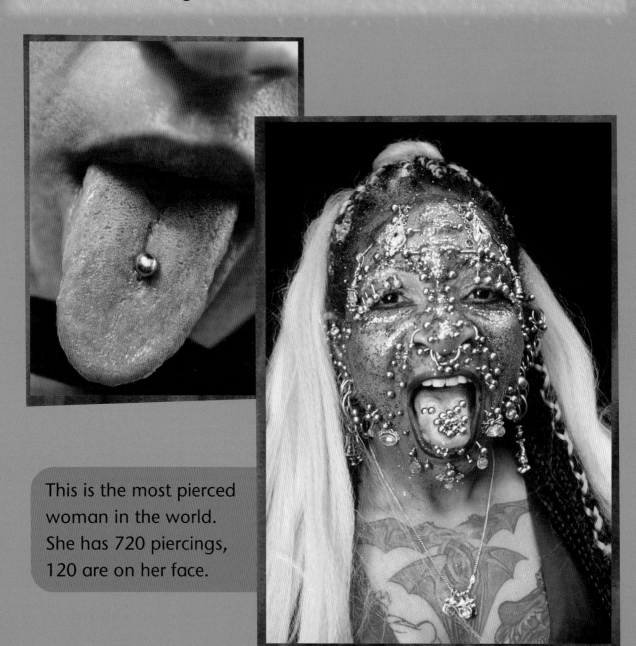

This is the most pierced woman in the world. She has 720 piercings, 120 are on her face.

Lip Plates

Read this passage.
Answer the questions on the next page.

Women in this tribe wear lip plates. Girls start to stretch their bottom lips the year before they get married. They make a hole and stretch it daily by rubbing it with butter and charcoal. Their two bottom front teeth are taken out to make room for the plate. The plates are made of clay or wood.

Ethiopia

Women wear their plates when there are men around. If they are alone, they take them off and their lower lip dangles down below their chin. A man pays a girl's father more goats to marry a girl with a big lip plate.

Think back to the text on page 21 and try to answer these questions.

1. Do women wear lip plates when they are little?

2. Why is it important to have a big lip plate?

3. Do the women wear the lip plates all the time?

In this tribe in Brazil it is the men who wear lip plates.

And Finally

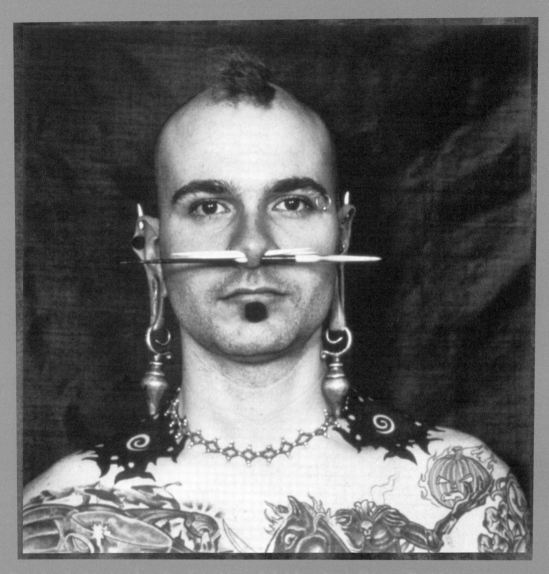

Look at this man. Can you list the
different kinds of body art he displays?

Answers

Jon has pierced ears, and a pierced nose.

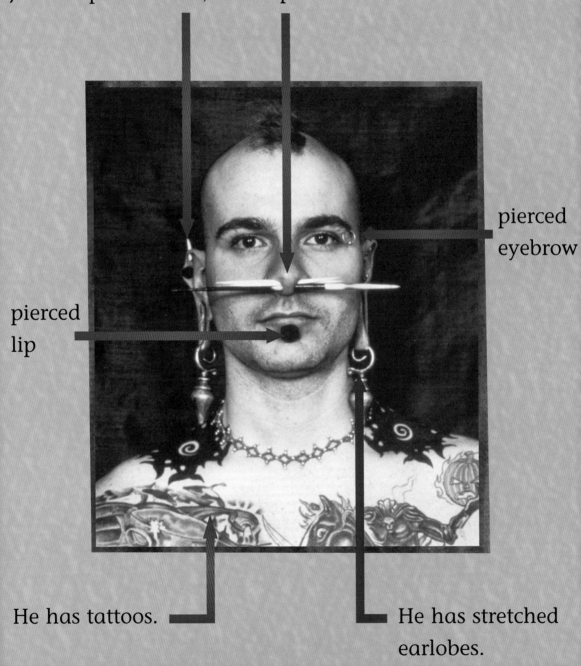

pierced eyebrow

pierced lip

He has tattoos.

He has stretched earlobes.